THE HAUNTED SCOTLAND COOKBOOK

Scottish Paranormal Book 2

By Alister Reid

BeulAithris
Publishing

Scotland

www.beul-aithris-publishing.com

ISBN 9781695082779

"A chef must think like a

Scientist

Plate like an

Artist

Work like a slave

Live like a warrior"

A.Reid
15/09/2019

Contents

Introduction

SCOTTIS   RMA

We are a
researcher
scientifi
exister

(C) Scottish Paranormal

Paranormal investigator and chef

Being a professional chef and a paranormal researcher and investigator are more similar than you may think. The late nights, unsociable hours, the physicality and use of energy, long hours, research, learning, patience, organization and all the demand. The list is almost endless you never stop learning and being needed! It's a nice feeling to have at times! And if we didn't would it all be worthwhile?

I have been fortunate enough to work with and brush shoulders with some of the highest-profile and well-respected figures in hospitality and the paranormal field. I have met some of the most incredible and amazingly influential people and been able to visit, investigate and work within some of the most amazing places only you could imagine or even dream of being allowed anywhere near. I don't put this down to good luck or fortune; it's simply working hard, dreaming and believing using your mind and train of thought, this is the most powerful tool known to man! You have to believe that things always happen for a reason, you just have to learn how to use them and negotiate your ladder in life. I don't believe in coincidences anymore.

I'm doing this book as a reflection of my experiences in both hospitality and the paranormal world along with the experiences I have encountered to date. As a professional chef, I have my whole life and career been somewhat of a self-proclaimed flavour technician, as well as a make it work kind of person: I will make it work, and it does! I can make things work and happen when I need to. It is almost like a manifestation in a weird and wonderful way.

If it doesn't work, I will find a way to make it work - it's similar to methods I use as a paranormal investigator for spiritual communication, don't stop until it works, and you get the answers and results you so desire. Everyone is different, there is always a way around everything and anything you just have to stop and be patient on occasions. Things don't always turn around at once; sometimes they do and sometimes they don't.

In this book, I want to share with you all the places I have visited, cooked, investigated and the people I have met on my journey so far. It's a hard task to start putting all this together. So, where do I start? Just before I take you on my journey, I want to tell you and share something with you. The mind is extremely powerful, and intention is key, put the intention out there! This helps you live an active and fun-filled lifestyle. Always be positive, if you follow these simple steps, opportunities will come, be negative and that is all you will attract. A positive mind is a healthy mind, always remove negativity, a beautiful life will blossom, and that's what this book is trying to demonstrate with my passion for food, paranormal, historic buildings and happy life. That we can all share and experience together.

I hope you enjoy this book as much as I have had writing it, Visiting and creating recipes and cooking in these haunted and historical locations. Meeting many amazing people and making friends along the way and not to mention all the centuries-old spirits who I have communicated with and met. These are memories that will last a lifetime and I thank you all deeply.

Many people have played an important part and roles in my thirty years to date, however only very few have given me the influences to succeed in life and I've used their wisdom to find the life skills and qualities to open the doors I needed. I keep a small close group of people around me, only the ones I can trust - it's how I work! I would firstly like to commemorate my grandparents from both sides of my family; they helped me form a real strong passion for food and life from an early age. Therefore, it is only fair I include some of their recipes in this haunted cookbook.

I would like to commemorate my close friends, and fellow paranormal researchers Gregor Stewart and Ryan O' Neill. Without their wisdom, I would not be writing this book, to begin with, the first people to give me the step into the paranormal world and believe in my methods and theories. Their knowledge, intelligence, and genuine personality are one of the greatest I have ever come across. Both are established authors and friends, whom without I would not be able to follow my pursuits. I would like to say a big thank you to these guys for just being you and always being there. Special thank you to all the guys at Scottish Paranormal my buddies and fellow investigators, Photo genius Kyle Stewart, app man Jonathan Garaway and Carrie O'Neill who makes all our merchandise, and all our group members, with special recognition to the SP subscribers who show such amazing support, My Scottish American buddy Rick McCallum! He inspired one of the many recipes in this book co-founder of Hollywood Ghost hunters and Professional

Stuntman and actor a genuine guy with so much personality. All my friends and family you know who you are - I can't mention you all. It's only fair I include two of my former head chefs! Many I have worked for and appreciate everything, but I have to say special thanks to two of them, Steve Johnston and David Kinnes, two traditionally old school chefs who have inspired many to happy cooking. But the most important thank you goes to my wife Gillian and our four amazing kids Abbey, Kenzie, Kieran and Sophie. Gillian does everything for me and our children I love you lots and I thank you for everything you do for us all.

Balgonie Castle

Celebration of The Winter Solstice Dinner with Scottish Paranormal and Balgonie Castle Scotland - myself with The Laird of Balgonie (R) and his son Stuart

We begin this journey with the historic and haunted Balgonie Castle situated near Milton of Balgonie, Fife, Scotland on the south bank of the River Leven. This is my personal favourite to investigate or even just visit a place of so much love and peacefulness. It's also a place I have experienced paranormal activity on many occasions to the extreme. Knocks, bangs, footsteps, shuffling, ice-cold breezes, high and low-temperature drops, static sounds, screams. There aren't many places inside Balgonie that you won't feel or experience something - after all, we are talking centuries worth of history.

Balgonie Castle is a defensive style castle that has welcomed many historical figures and people over the centuries, including royalty. Mary, Queen of Scots is believed to have stayed at Balgonie Castle on her way to Wemyss Castle where she would meet Henry Stuart, styled as Lord Darnley. The two would later marry. King James IV visited on the 20th August 1496 on his way to St Andrews. Others such as the infamous Rob Roy MacGregor paid Balgonie a visit in January 1716 with some two hundred clansmen and prisoners. The castle was believed to have been unoccupied on his siege and he only stayed two days causing much damage to the castle and emptying its wine cellar. Another documented visitor to the castle is that of Dr. Benjamin Rush, a signatory of the American Declaration of Independence. Daniel Defoe, famous for the novel Robinson Crusoe, also paid the castle a visit.

The castle itself dates to the 14th century: records indicate that the castle was built around the 1360s by the Sibbald family who had held the lands of Balgonie for around some one hundred years or more prior to laying the foundations of Balgonie Castle. It's possible the lands around Balgonie may be that of a former Pictish Kingdom. The Great Tower was built for Sir Thomas Sibbald of Balgonie in the 1360s who was at the time King Edward III's Treasurer. This is the oldest standing building within the castle and is the oldest complete occupied tower in Fife and one of the best examples of architecture in Scotland. Later Additions and remodels to the castle were added by Sir Robert Lundie in 1496 who built the now ruinous north range.

Sir Robert was a courtier of King James IV and much of what is seen at Balgonie today was added around this period. Another Famous Laird of the castle and central its development is Alexander Leslie 1st Earl of Leven. An extremely successful military man rising to Field Marshal in the Swedish army and on his return to Scotland Lord General of the Covenanter Army of Scotland and later Lord of both Kingdoms of Scotland and England. He died at Balgonie Castle 4th April 1661 aged 78 years old. His spirit is believed to still wander the castle; the most famous incident was when the Lairds wife had been resting within the Great Hall. She opened her eyes to see the apparition of a bearded man standing looking at her in what she described as 17th Century clothes! Could this have been the 1st Earl of Leven letting her know he is still around?

Balgonie's most famous resident is Green Jeanie or Green Jean. Her apparition is most commonly seen walking across the old north block ruins. She is said to be the ghost of an extremely beautiful young lady. It is not documented exactly who she might be but one of the theories we believe is that she is the daughter of a former Laird of the castles. Records are extremely hard to come by as we are talking around the turn of the 15th Century towards the early 16th century. From our research, we believe this to be the same spirit that has been sighted at nearby Macduff's Castle, Wemyss Castle and most commonly, The Ancient Wemyss caves. It's possible that this is the apparition of Mary Sibbald who tragically died from a broken heart after being falsely accused of theft. Perhaps her memories lie within all these locations. It's believed she may have also shown herself in Balgonie's tower one evening very recently.

Sightings also include a ghostly monk or priest lurking near the fully restored ancient chapel area. A wounded soldier is seen walking the courtyard before disappearing into the wall or perhaps a former doorway. There is said to be upwards of at least twelve active spirits within Balgonie Castle other sightings include that of a bodiless head! Seen floating on the staircase with a ruffle around its neck. Ghostly dogs are also witnessed around the castle.

I am delighted to be dedicating this recipe to the present Laird of Balgonie Castle, Raymond Stanley Morris Laird of Balgonie and Eddergoll. A true gentleman he has spent so much of his life dedicated to his castle and its restoration for us to see it as we see it today and protecting its future for many years to come.

"The Lairds Scone recipe must only be used under the approval of the Laird of Balgonie castle. It's also tradition the first scone cut must be the largest and given to the laird for his approval."

A.Reid 22/03/2019

The Lairds Scone of Balgonie Castle

This recipe was created and inspired by Alister Reid in recognition dedication and tribute to Raymond Stanley Morris the Laird of Balgonie & Eddergoll

The Main Tower at Balgonie Castle, one of the oldest and complete towers standing in Scotland

Ingredients
100g Golden Castor Sugar
100g Full Fat Salted Butter
500g Sieved Self-Raising Flour
2 Free Range Eggs
180ml Semi Skimmed Milk

1 Fresh Vanilla Pod
200g White Chocolate
100g Raw & Peeled Pistachio Nuts
200g Fresh Tarvit Home Farm Cupar Raspberries

Method

Preheat oven to 180°C. Rub together butter, flour, sugar until they have a crumble resemblance. Whisk together the eggs and milk until combined, add in in vanilla bean seeds, roughly break half-white chocolate and add to the flour mix. Make a well in the middle of the mix and gently pour in egg mixture, with a wooden spoon gradually combine the flour until all mixed in, do not over mix. Tip the mix onto a heavily floured surface, add raspberries and gently knead together when combined gently press out dough evenly until about half the thickness of an index finger, then cut into triangles, carefully place on a baking tray, and bake at 180°C for fifteen minutes or until golden brown and crisp. Once cool melt chocolate over a Bain Marie, drizzle onto scones and sprinkle with grounded Pistachio, serve with the Lairds favourite lashings of butter

The Lairds Scone of Balgonie Castle

Hollywood Ghost Hunters in Mary Kings Close

Hollywood Ghost Hunter Rick McCallum and Kyle Stewart During a visit to Slains Castle, Cruden Bay, Aberdeenshire

During the sunny summer month of June, Ryan, Greg and I hit haunted and historic St Andrews a seaside town steeped in history and famous for its many golf courses and sandy beaches. St Andrews is the home of golf. Known famously for its University founded in 1413, along with its famous landmarks including its great cathedral, castle, and chapels to name just a few.

We walked along Murray Park to pick up our guest for the day, Rick. As we approached his hotel, we all looked forward, a little in anticipation, to meeting this gentle giant for the first time! However, within seconds we knew he was pretty cool. Rick began his stunt career in 1982 performing a fight scene with Chuck Norris and has gone on to over eighty plus credits to his name including appearances with Clint Eastwood and Kane Hodder, also known as Jason in the *Friday the 13th* franchise. He co-founded Hollywood Ghost hunters with best friend Kane Hodder along with R.A Mihailoff and Danielle Harris.

Rick spends much of his time in between filming and ghost hunting travelling across the world. He has a propounded soft spot for what he calls his spiritual home Scotland.

We have had many great adventures with Rick across Scotland, including a haunted Ireland road trip at the beginning of 2019 where we investigated the Hell Fire Club at Montpellier Hill outside Dublin and the infamous Leap Castle in County Offally, home to some of the most notorious ghost stories on the planet. Rick is a very calm and respectful investigator he sticks to the basic methods and trusted techniques when investigating. We have a saying - when Rick's about then spirit is about.

Rick favours his trusted K-11 when investigating and he has a fantastic connection to yes and no answers by allowing spirit to manipulate the lights on the device. A K-11 is an EMF meter, measuring the electromagnetic field in the surrounding area. It is believed spirit might influence the magnetic field to provide possible readings via the device; it should be noted that there should not be any live wires or devices nearby, including mobile phones that could affect the K- 11, as any of these in the close proximity of the device can provide false readings.

Rick has investigated some of the highest-profile haunted locations across America and in fact, the world, but I want to share an investigation with you closer to home in the deep dark Edinburgh underground.

Mary King's Close is a historic claustrophobic close located in Scotland's Capital underneath the Royal Mile in the Old Town area of Edinburgh. A true relic of Edinburgh's insanitary past, the close is believed to have been named after Mary King a former Merchant Burgess who live in the close in the 17th century. The streets themselves are believed to date from the early 16th century. The close was closed and almost forgotten about in the 18th century when the Royal Exchange was built closing of all access to the public. Many myths, legends, and stories abound of hauntings from those who enter Mary King's Close. Research suggests the close might have come together from many other closes and streets but is now effectively-known and preserved as a tourist attraction in the city.

Mary King's Close has many reported hauntings dating back from as early as the 17th century; these include the ghost of Annie a child who is believed to have died in the close. The most famous tale related to Annie is of when a Japanese psychic visited the close in 1992. The psychic was unimpressed by her tour until she entered the small rooms of the close where she was overcome with the feelings of sickness, hunger, and coldness. When she tried to leave the room, she felt the feeling of an unseen presence tugging and pulling on her leg, which she described as being a small child who had been left to die by her family. This was the beginning of Annie's room. When you visit this room today, you will find it packed full of teddies and gifts from around the world left as an offering for Annie.

Other famous residents of the close include Mr. Chesney the last person to leave the close in 1897. A saw maker by trade, he lived and worked in the close, where his workshop was located next to his home at the bottom of Mary King's Close. Strange noises, knocks, bangs, and footsteps are heard in and around his house, its apparent Mr. Chesney might have returned to the close where he lived all his life.

I want to share my experiences on my first visit to Mary King's Close in the summer of 2018. Rick had invited Ryan and me along for a joint group investigation with some of his friends from down south; these included Spirit Medium Gary Fields And Anubis Paranormal. It was a calm and relaxed summer night and very warm, as I remember not needing a jacket. We were later arrivals to the close as I had been working. As we entered, we could see the guys already deep into investigating.

I was instantly in awe of the sites in front of my eyes. Ryan who had investigated the close on many occasions beforehand had warned me about the activity I could potentially experience. Did I believe him? Well, I didn't doubt him but at the same time, sometimes things are so massively hyped up so much it falls short of everyone's expectations. Thankfully, on this visit, I was not disappointed and had still my best paranormal encounter to date.

We joined up with Rick and the guys in Annie's room where they had been experiencing some cold spots, temperature drops, bangs and taps that we could not find any natural causes for. Further into the session, we heard what we think might have been a girl's voice! Could this have been Annie letting us know she was around? I joined Rick in the corridor with Ryan and Craig to conduct some EMF communication on the K-11 and instantly we had contact from spirit. It was at this point I moved up to the back of the small passageway to stand behind Ryan and look for further readings. As we all stood still in silence we heard what could only be described as a young child running over our heads above. Bear in mind there was a atone floor above our heads and further up was the City Chambers that were locked up as it was 2 am on a Saturday morning.

Unbelievably we all just looked at each other in complete shock as to what we had just experienced. I have never had such validation physically before, after or since. This was not the end either - as the night went on, we experienced doors opening by themselves, as well as hearing them slamming closed and more unseen footsteps and whispers. When I returned eight months later on a team investigation the close manager said they had not had such activity since. One of my best nights investigating and something we still talk about regularly. So it's only fair I personally dedicated this recipe to Rick for what still my best night investigating and what else could I create other than his favourite comfort food of burgers.

Ps, the Recipe includes Haggis! Rick does not like Haggis! But will forced to eat it before leaving the table in the fashion of a true Scot!

Wise Words A. Reid 28/3/2019

Rick and Ally at St. Andrews Cathedral during a Scottish Paranormal History Tour hosted By Gregor Stewart

The "McCallum" Burger

This recipe was created and inspired by Alister Reid in recognition of my dear friend Rick McCallum

Rick enjoying his Burger @ 1B Westport Cupar Scotland. Note his trusty K-11 on the table

Ingredients
500g Minced Angus Beef
200g Braised Beef Shin
100g Streaky Bacon
2 Small Finely Diced Red Onions
1 Diced Red Chilli
1 Free Range Egg
1 Tsp Dijon Mustard
1 Tsp BBQ Sauce
100g Fresh Breadcrumbs
Salt/Ground Pepper
100g Blue Cheese

Method
Pre-heat oven to 180°C. Sweat the onions with a little oil over medium heat until translucent and beginning to colour, add in the chillies and gently cook for one minute. Remove from the heat and set aside to cool. In a large metal

bowl add in the minced beef along with the breadcrumbs, onions and chillies and eggs mix together until combined, add in the mustard, BBQ sauce and season accordingly. Make a little test burger to check the mix is to your taste. Split the mix into four large burgers and press to your desired thickness. Place in refrigerator for an hour to chill and let the flavour develop. Meanwhile, shred the braised beef and heat up with a little gravy. On a chargrill or in a pre-heated frying pan, sear the burgers on both sides until coloured. Whilst this is happening, place the streaky bacon strips on a grill bar tray and cook until crispy. Drizzle some honey over the bacon for ultimate sweetness. When juices begin to appear on top of the burger flip over and cook until the juices reappear on top (this will make the burgers "medium"), place on an ovenproof tray and spoon the braised beef onto the burgers. Place slices of the blue cheese and crispy bacon onto the burgers and stack one on top of the other place in oven until cheese has melted or if you like your burger more well-done leave a little longer. Rick likes his burger pink in the middle! Serve how you desire. For the ultimate "McCallum Burger" serve with iceberg lettuce, beef tomato, toasted pretzel pun, homemade onion rings, double-cooked Rooster Chips, and top with a haggis bonbon.

The "McCallum Burger"

My son, Kenzie, with Rick ghost hunting haunted castles

Crawford Priory and Lady Mary Crawford

Crawford Priory, Springfield, Near Cupar, Fife, Scotland

Lady Mary Crawford's apparition is said to wander the grounds of this spectacular gothic-style building, hidden deep within the county of Fife, Crawford Priory is a stunning Gothic mansion that was constructed to its current style around 1809, sitting upon an earlier building that was named Crawford Lodge (1758). These lands belonged to the Lindsay-Crawford family and would find themselves in the hands of Lady Mary Lindsay Crawford around 1808. The priory sits around two miles south-west of Cupar, next to the village of Springfield. Its older stables are now complete redeveloped as stunning houses nestled within the estate.

Lady Crawford was often described as strange by some, she never married for one thing and she had an amazing love for animals, preferring their company to that of most people. Some say she was highly religious, but the wonderment here is whether highly religious or highly spiritual which are rather different approaches. She is said to have had a rather large menagerie of animals at Crawford Priory. She was also particularly fond of a small deer too. There is a pet cemetery to the rear of the Priory with headstones to all her pets. She was so fond of every single pet, that her will left adequate funds to look after them all. Her pets were, however, a little less fond of the spirits that walked Crawford Priory prior to the passing of Lady Crawford.

We as Scottish Paranormal have uncovered information with the help of our followers, friends, and contacts concerning the property while Lady Crawford was alive and living here. Lady Mary Lindsay-Crawford often, as has been told, was in the company of spirits herself. She did not mind these at all, and most likely embraced it fully. Some of her pets however did not like the extra company. On occasion, they would refuse to enter a room if the spirits were about or, would walk on one side of the many corridors if a spirit was coming the other way.

One of our friends has reported to us that as a child she heard that one particular cat would not pass through a set of double doors. It would take a run-up to the open doors and he would jump in. The cat in question would walk through all other doors, just not this particular one. So who or what was lingering and causing such behaviour in Lady Crawford's pets?

It has been suggested that the spirit of a past butler may be the cause, still wandering the corridors and rooms of this Gothic building, another suggestion is that the spirit is that of one of the Lindsay-Crawford family, possibly the brother who may still also be attached to this property. This is an area we hope we can gain answers, possibly through our ITC Techniques from inside the ruins of this property. Lady Crawford passed to spirit in 1833 leaving her splendid property, her pets, and the lands behind. Or did she? As reports were quick to surface about a white apparition floating gracefully through the house and surrounding land as if in search of something, some suggested it was in-fact, Lady Crawford herself.

Was she in search of her beloved pets? This certainly seems to be the suggestion. Kyle Stewart had an eerie occurrence here, in the area between both the Priory and Lady Crawford's final resting place at Lady Mary Wood. It was next to a bad corner that has a track going up to the burial area where visitors may park their cars. In the shadow of the woods on that rather strange spooky night, Kyle witnessed what can only be described as a white apparition of a lady standing there, with a shroud on and no shoes on her feet. Of course, this startled him as he drove past! This was during late spring and early summer at around 10.30 pm, when he was cutting through this way to go home, after dropping a friend off. He does recall long dark hair and although it was night-time, it was a lightish night. He could not shake the image and did not look back after passing, such was his shock. Incidentally, a mere months later

Kyle's Dad, Greg Stewart, was driving past this exact same area when all his electrics in the car just died, only to recover as he got further along the road around said bad corner.

Was this again Lady Crawford making her presence known? How many others have seen her apparition here and not come forward for fear of ridicule? This takes me onto a story I was told by Ryan O'Neill around 2005 where a friend of a friend was driving past the crossroads at Springfield near the estate. He too said he witnessed a white apparition floating through the area, so much so, he high tailed it out of there fast. Connected? I think it is and it seems either Lady Crawford is not at rest - possibly due to vandals attacking her property and burial site, or we have a non-sentient replay. I think it may be the first reason, however due to multiple sightings and different areas.

Another story comes from a couple who used to live in the old stable block.

"We were having coffee in the lounge when what appeared to be a female walked in then out. We both saw this, and we ran down the stairs to see who it was. We found no one."

Again, is this Lady Crawford, and was she looking for her beloved horses. On the other hand, perhaps she is just checking her old locations and letting people know she is here.

The building itself is now in a sad state of disrepair and extremely dangerous. Extra precaution should be taken and its best not to enter the building for your own safety. I would like to tribute this recipe to Lady Mary Crawford and her once-grand home the inspiration behind this story is the surrounding fields full of oats and with the local oat mill being close what better recipe to produce a recipe for the area itself

"A place of such beauty that nature is slowly reclaiming"

A.Reid 18/06/2018

Lady Crawford's Flap Jack

This recipe was created and inspired by Alister Reid in recognition, dedication and tribute to Lady Mary Crawford

Inside the ruins of Crawford Priory

Ingredients
400g Unsalted Butter
150g Earl Grey Soaked Sultanas
200g Golden Syrup
2 Oranges (Juiced & Zested)
200g Light Soft Brown Sugar
500g Quaker Porridge Oats
200g Plain Flour
1 Juice Of A Lemon
4 Tbsp. Rum

Method

Preheat oven to 150°C. Soak sultanas overnight by placing them in a container, add two Earl Grey tea bags and cover with boiling water leave to infuse and cool down. Gently squeeze the sultanas to remove some of the excess juice then place in a pan with the orange juice and zest and add in the rum gently simmer until the orange has absorbed slightly then put aside in a warm place to soak up the orange and rum. In another pan, place the syrup, butter, lemon juice, and sugar and heat gently until the butter has melted and the sugar has dissolved. Do not over stir the mixture then set aside. Mix the flour and oats in a large bowl then add in the syrup mixture along with the sultanas any excess juices. Make sure the mixture is well mixed then tip into a large greaseproof lined tin and spreading out evenly and gently press flat, place in the preheated oven for 20-30 minutes until golden remove and gently press with a flat greased pallet knife. Leave to cool drizzle with icing or melted chocolate cut into squares and serve. Flapjacks can be stored in a sealed container in the fridge for up to two weeks.

Slains Castle, Bram Stoker

Slains Castle, Cruden Bay, Aberdeenshire

Slains Castle, Aberdeenshire lies upon the rugged clifftops of Cruden Bay, looking over the North Sea. Slains is also known as "New Slains Castle" to differentiate from "Old Slains". The original new castle was built in the 16th Century by the 9th Earl of Erroll, Francis Hay to replace Old Slains six miles further southwest. The lands of Slains were held by the Clan Hay family for over 300 years, since the 14th century when King James II made Sir William Hay Earl of Errol. Originally called Bowness before latterly being renamed New Slains, the castle was built out from a Square tower house and courtyard before being remodelled drastically over the following centuries. The Hay family ended their 300-year ownership of the castle in 1913 when the 20th Earl sold the Castle to Sir John Ellerman a multi-millionaire Shipping Director who leased out the castle during his ownership. In 1925, the roof was removed from the castle to avoid tax-paying purposes leaving the derelict granite shell as we see it today.

In 2004, it was reported the Slains Partnership was preparing plans for restorations, turning the castle into 35-holiday apartments. The scheme was granted outline planning permission in 2007 by Aberdeenshire Council but the plans were put on hold in 2009 due to the economic downturn of the recession that hit that year. No further reports of development have been reported and is now a top tourist attraction for the passing tourist.

Slains Castle is known worldwide for many reasons not just for its paranormal activity and its uncared-for historic status, but during its glory years, this was once a place where celebrities of the time would be entertained, celebrate, wined and dined. Perhaps today one of its most well-known visitors was that of Mr. Bram Stoker! Many commonly refer to Slains Castle as the possible inspiration behind the novel of *Dracula* (1887). Bram Stoker was a regular visitor to the area and was believed to have also stayed in the castle during one particular visit. Local history and facts Suggest Bram would sit in his favourite guesthouse along in Cruden Bay, The Kilmarnock Arms Hotel and peer out the window along the cliffs to Slains Castle. Was this where Bram perhaps first found his inspiration to inspire a global enterprise of Dracula?

He is said to have had a 17-year love affair with the Cruden Bay area and this was where the story of the famous vampire would emerge. A high profile author of the time he would seek the shelter of Scotland and Cruden bay to get away from the publicity of his hometown Dublin. Local folklore suggests that even Draculas infamous fangs could have come from the jagged rocks on the cliff face

It is no real surprise that Slains has such an appealing draw for so many reasons and visitors alike. A hot spot for paranormal activity is also reported within the granite skeletal shell that remains. Though it may no longer be the power and fortress it once was but uninhabited for almost a century, it still is home to many wandering lost souls of years gone by. Sightings include ghostly World War Two soldiers marching past the castle; this could be from the possible underground bunkers located close to the castle.

A phantom horse and cart are reported to thunder along the side of the castle and through the gates to its former courtyard before disappearing. A ghostly White Lady has also been reported screaming in pain from perhaps a form of torture or regret or perhaps even false imprisonment? She is believed to have been falsely accused of being and for crimes she did not commit witch by her lover, and as a result, her spirit still wanders the ruins seeking help.

The 21st Earl of Errol Victor Hay is also said to wander the ruins of his once glorious home perhaps looking for some unfinished business. The most compelling evidence though I have come across was a photograph captured by my fellow friend and investigator Kyle Stewart, who caught a picture next to one of the ruined towers in the former courtyard stable block. He capture reveals what appears to be a ghostly monk standing and perhaps even glaring back at the camera; it is a bone-chilling piece of evidence. This area of the courtyard seems to be an extremely active hot spot for sightings and activity it's certainly a place no one should enter alone after dusk.

*"You can feel and hear the sea wind,
the waves crashing of the rugged
coastal rocks, it's beautiful in itself"*

A. Reid 14/5/2018

The Slains Buttery
Created by Alister Reid to Slains Castle & the inspiration f Bram Stokers novel

Main Corridor Slains Castle

Ingredients
500g Strong Plain Bread Flour
400g Unsalted Butter
1 Tbsp. Soft Light Brown Sugar
350ml Tepid Water
9g Dried Yeast
1 Tbsp. Salt
1 Stick Stornoway Black Pudding
6 Streaky Bacon Rashers

Method
In a large bowl, mix the flour, yeast, sugar, and salt until combined. Make a small well in the centre of the mix, gradually pour in the water slowly whilst combining mixture with a wooden spoon, until the mixture comes together as a sticky dough. (You may not need to use all the water). Turn the dough out

onto a lightly floured work surface and knead for 6-8 minutes until smooth and elastic. Place the dough into a clean, lightly greased bowl and cover with cling film. Set aside in a warm place to prove for at least one hour, and doubled in size, knock back and allow to rise again. In a separate bowl, cream the butter until soft and velvety Divide the mixture into four equal portions. Turn out the dough onto a lightly floured surface and knead for a further one minute. Roll out the dough to about one cm thick. Spread one portion of the butter over a quarter of the dough edge and fold it over. Do this with the opposite side. Spread over half side of the mix and again fold over and spread the last butter over half the dough fold over and roll out once more to one cm thick. Preheat the oven to 200°C. Cut the dough into 16 pieces and roll each into a round, flat bun Transfer the buns to a lightly oiled baking tray and set aside for 40-45 minutes, or until they have doubled in size again; leave enough space between for expansion. Bake them in the oven for 15 minutes, or until they have risen and golden-brown and cooked through. Set aside to cool on a wire rack. Serve warm with lashings of butter, grilled Stornoway black pudding, and streaky bacon. For an extra vampire bloody twist, add some homemade Tomato ketchup

Bannockburn House, Bonnie Prince Charlie

Bannockburn House, Bannockburn, Stirlingshire, Scotland

Bannockburn House is a historic country mansion in Bannockburn, Stirlingshire. As an A listed building, this house is an extremely historically significant property. The house is located within close proximity to the location of the battle of Bannockburn (1314) where Scottish King Robert the Bruce famously defeated the army of King Edward II during the first wars of Scottish Independence. Bannockburn house was built in the late 17th Century and was most likely commissioned by Sir Hugh Patterson.

The house changed hand numerous times over the next three centuries where further additions and remodelling of the house took place. During the latter part of the 20th century, the house became somewhat unoccupied and slowly fell into disrepair and a former shadow of its former self. The glorious house was placed on the market for sale in February 2016. The house attracted much attention including TV coverage and many keen high profile investors. With much help and fundraising in the local community, the Save Bannockburn House Trust was thankfully born and in April 2017, the Trust secured exclusives rights to purchase the house and safeguard its future for the community, and future generations and the people of Scotland. In November

2017 the funds required had been raised via a mixture of fundraising, public money, and grants. Bannockburn's immediate future was now safeguarded.

Both Sir Hugh's son and grandson were both made Baronets of the house. It was during this time that the "Great Pretender" a certain young Charles Edward Stuart stayed at the house in early 1746 prior to the Battle of Culloden during the last Jacobite rebellion; he was building his army for a battle to put a Stuart back on the Scottish Throne. It's believed this is where the "Bonnie Prince" first met his lover and mother of his child Clementina Walkinshaw. It's believed the Prince spent the night of the 14th September at the house and it is said that there was a specific reason for his visit and stay in the house prior to his taking of Edinburgh in the following days. It is not sure exactly why he visited but many believe this could be him paying command to Patterson, who had shown his support to the cause of the 1715 Jacobite Rebellion with the Prince's father, the "Old Pretender" James Francis Edward Stuart. The house with so many grand rooms and ceilings, style and décor, adequately has a room named the "Bonnie Prince Charlies room" that boasts a fantastic and vintage four-poster bed. Rumour has it this is possibly the bed the prince might have slept in during his visit to Bannockburn house.

The house has also had its fair shares of tragedies over the years including a fire-raising by arsonists in the 1970s that ripped through one of the wings. Thankfully, the fire was kept to one room and the house survived. Visible damage of this can still be seen but renovations to restore the room and make it inhabitable again have now taken place. With so much history and so many secrets including the mysterious door locked safe with no key, it's no wonder it's a hot spot for reported paranormal activity. The outline of a female apparition was seen during one of the few conducted paranormal nights that have taken place at this location. This happened in the balcony area. Volunteers and workmen are said to have caught fleeting glimpses of shadows and movement while working here. The feelings of Bannockburn house – being watched, silently, from within the amazing house are also reported. Other able investigators from within Scotland have successfully used communication techniques here to tap into the energies present. Other reports from various sources include phenomena such as doors opening and closing, Staff at times feeling watched, various loud bangs and knocks, live audio captures.

During a private team investigation in May 2018, Greg Stewart and I witnessed the tell-tale signs of REAL paranormal manifestation. While conducting a session in the kitchen, we were met with an icy blast as if something was hovering over our shoulders and we felt as if we were physically pushed from within the doorway. Was this the former gardener who liked to antagonise vulnerable women? We had to move such was the power of this activity. The last Scottish Paranormal public event here was wild. It took place in the summer of 2018 when females were heavily affected by something. They had to be taken out of the session and looked after carefully. We had to have three members of the public carried out the last time we visited the house. One thing is for sure this house holds energy and should not be taken lightly in the night time hours.

What better way to pay tribute to one Bannockburn house's most famous visitors, Bonnie Prince Charlie with a nice, simple but almost royal feeling classic recipe? Liked or not by many he is still one of my favourite Scottish historical figures and fittingly deserves a little remembrance of what perhaps could have been.

"A strikingly overwhelming house full of character and a real feeling of grand and great importance."

A. Reid 12/11/2018

The Young Pretender Hot Cross Bun

This recipe was created and inspired by Alister Reid in recognition to Charles Edward Stuart and The Bannockburn House Trust

The Young Pretender Hot Cross Bun in preparation

Ingredients
Buns

600ml Semi Skimmed Milk
100g Butter
1kg Strong Bread Flour
150g Golden Caster Sugar
2 Tbsp. Vegetable Oil
14g Dried Yeast
2 Beaten Eggs

150g Tea Soaked Sultanas
5g Ground Cinnamon
100g Mixed Peel
Zest - 1 Orange
2 Pink Lady Apples
5g Salt

Cross

75g Plain Flour and Water

The Young Pretender" Hot Cross Bun

Method

Heat oven to 220°C. Bring the milk to the boil, remove from the heat and add butter. Leave to cool until it reaches hand temperature. Put the strong bread flour, salt, caster sugar, and yeast into a bowl. Make a well in the centre. Pour in the warm milk and butter mixture, then add the egg gently and gradually, using a wooden spoon, mix to bring everything together until you have a sticky dough. Tip on to a lightly floured surface and knead the dough for five minutes until smooth and elastic. Put the dough in a lightly greased clean bowl. Cover with cling film and leave to rise in a warm place for 1 hr until doubled in size Tip in sultanas, mixed peel, zest of orange, finely chopped apple and ground cinnamon. Knead into the dough, make sure the ingredients are distributed evenly through the dough Leave to rise for another hour or until doubled in size make sure the dough is always covered. Cut the dough and weigh into 70g pieces. Roll into a smooth ball on a clean surface. Arrange the buns side by side on a baking tray leaving a little gap for expansion, but I like them slightly touching when risen so you can tear them apart when fresh. Set aside to rise for another hour and then with the plain flour add a few drops of water and mix into a paste that is spreadable and place into a piping bag, pipe along the buns and then the opposite way to form crosses Bake for 20 minutes in the middle of the oven, until golden brown. Remove from oven when ready and glaze with some warm apricot jam with a pastry brush and glaze the buns this must be done when the buns are still warm. Allow the buns to cool, and then cut open and serve toasted with homemade orange marmalade

Dreel Halls. St. Adrian of May and the Accused Witches

Dreel Halls Tower (C) Kyle Stewart

The Dreel Halls sit on the shorelines in the heart of Anstruther, Fife, Scotland. There has been a parish church sited on this historic and holy site for at least ten centuries! This site was first dedicated to St Ethernan of May; his name was later Latinised from Ethernan to Adrian. Saint Adrian was believed to have been murdered by Vikings around circa 870. Local legend has it that his body floated across the sea from the May Island in a stone coffin and landed on the shores that the Dreel halls now sit.

His coffin is still visible today in the graveyard sited beside the Dreel Halls and is visible through a glass lid chamber. It's believed he might have also been a bishop of St Andrews, he is commemorated on the 3rd of December. Very little is known about the life of Ethernan or Adrian but he may have been an Irish Monk or Bishop. He possibly left St Andrews to seek the hermitage he preferred and set up new monasteries including on the May Island. He possibly fled St Andrews during the Viking raids, which would eventually catch up with him, and his monasteries on the island where the Vikings would slaughter the entire population and leave the Island abandoned for centuries.

Dreel Halls Main entrance (C)Kyle Stewart

The land the Dreel Halls now sit developed out of many other churches. One of the original churches was founded and built around the time of 1243. The church was extremely large and was sited over the existing graveyard we see today. The original church tower had a brazier that blazed on the roof to navigate ships into the harbour shores: this was one of the first of its kind in Scotland. It was later replaced with a replica tower on May Island. Damage followed the church in a fiery sermon from notorious preacher John Knox in 1559. It also suffered vandalism from English soldiers in 1651. During a horrific storm in 1670, part of the surrounding grounds gave way and made the harbour unusable.

Without the harbour, the importance of the burgh declined and the church was gradually made much smaller but it remained in use. The surrounding graveyard still contains much interest in Scottish history. Although much smaller than its original size, noticeable gravestones and burials can still be found including the grave of George Dishington, one of a local family descended from King Robert the Bruce's sister. Also buried here is Mathew Forster Conolly a local author, lawyer and was responsible for the first bank to be founded in Anstruther.

The result of the importance of this burial site in previous centuries was that when the Sexton would dig a new grave he could uncover as many as six skulls at any one time. The well was uncovered during excavations and building work in the 19th century. The Dreel Halls is now in community ownership and is used for many social events and clubs its currently in phase two of its refurbishment and is due to reopen in late 2019.

It's, therefore, no surprise that the land and building hold so much energy for potential paranormal activity. Saint Nicholas Tower within the Dreel Halls has seen its fair share of activities. During recent research and investigations, Scottish Paranormal found an interesting witch connection. It was our very own Gregor Stewart who would first visit the Dreel Halls on business to do a historical talk in early 2016. Greg asked out of curiosity if he could place one of his devices at the top of the 16th century tower to see if he could record any possible paranormal activity. With a fully charged battery, he placed his device down and pressed record only to return a slight time later to see the device completely drained of energy and no evidence captured. This is a common occurrence in the field of paranormal research. It played on Greg's mind for the next couple of years until one day Ryan O' Neil was driving past and mentioned the Halls to Greg. It was then that Greg decided we would try contacting the Trust to allow us access to the ancient church site.

We would not be disappointed - upon entering the 16th century tower, you are blessed to see the original stonework and spiral stone staircase. Immediate cold spots, temperature fluctuations, and EMF spike detection hit us. During a live-recorded ICT test communication session using one of our FM sweep radio devices Coultus Box, we had contacted what we believed to be a male spirit. After asking for formal validation and what he did, we would be left speechless and gobsmacked and in stone-cold fear! Bear in mind we had been in the tower and were surrounded with thick stone walls. This made it extremely difficult for any radio reception to be received. The response we would get in a clear broad Scottish accent, "Killed her" confirmed our beliefs that a young accused witch had been held within the towers cells and murdered by this man.

For the rest of the investigation, we would feel the energy of an intimidating presence surrounded by mixed emotions of fear and extreme sadness. It's believed that up to three known accused witches had been held at Dreel Halls during the notorious Scottish witch trials of the 16th century onwards. Further analysing and research followed this investigation and we would find the following names who we believe might have been held in the tower at the Dreel Halls. They are as follows: Agnes Melville, circa 1594; Agnes Anstruther, 1613; Isobel Dairsie, 1643; and Elizabeth Dick, 1701. During further research and communication, we heard words such as "witch", "prick" "marks" - all words used during the witch trials. We also believe there to be a young child present, along with a former minister who is still perhaps performing his ceremonies. Records state that Anstruther Western Tollbooth was, in fact, the Dreel Halls.

I've decided with the "East Nuek of Fife" being so famous for its fishing that it's only right I do a fish-based recipe with fish being also smoked locally what better way to celebrate a recipe of such localness, fresh and homely

"Walking into the Tower within Dreel Halls is like a Step back through the centuries"

A. Reid 22/01/2019

Dreel Halls Fishcake

This recipe was created and inspired by Alister Reid in dedication to St. Adrian and the accused Witches of Anstruther West

The Dreel Halls Fishcake

Ingredients
400g Dry Mashed Potatoes
150g Natural Boneless Smoked Haddock
100g Fine Diced Onion
Handful Chopped Chives
1 Sliced Spring Onion
2 Large Free-Range Egg
400g Fresh Homemade Breadcrumbs
Vegetable Oil
Unsalted Soft Butter
1 Organic Lemon
Salt And Pepper
Plain Flour

Method

In a pan place the haddock fillets and cover with milk or bring to a gentle boil then turn off the heat but leave the fish to cool in the liquor. Place the potatoes in a pan and cover with cold water and a pinch of salt. Bring to a gentle boil, boil until tender and a knife goes through them then drain and place back in the pan. Over low heat allow some more of the moisture to evaporate add in salt and pepper, a generous amount of butter and some of the liquor you have cooked the fish in - adding this maximises the flavour then mash until smooth! Set aside until needed later. Sweat the finely diced onions with a little butter and vegetable oil until translucent and beginning to brown turn the heat off and add in the haddock breaking it up into flakes, then add in the sliced spring onions, chives. Gently beat up one egg then add into this mix and combine. Squeeze some of the lemon juice into the mix and then in a large bowl combine the mixture with the mashed potatoes. Add some plain flour and mix until you can mould a round shape to your size requirements, set on a tray and place in the refrigerator until firm. Get three trays and place some plain flour in one and the breadcrumbs in another. Beat the egg with some milk and place it into the other tray. Lightly roll the fishcake in the flour, shaking off any excess and dip into the egg mixture and then the breadcrumbs until evenly coated. Gently heat a frying pan with oil and place in your fishcakes, turning halfway through cooking until golden brown. Transfer to an ovenproof dish and finish in a pre-heated oven at 180°C until cooked through and piping hot, then serve with a nice salad and a soft poached egg or with some crushed peas and chilli sauce.

Govan Shipyard, the Fairfield Museum

Fairfeld Museum, Govan Shipyard Glasgow, Scotland

Voted one of Glasgow's most admired buildings, this iconic, A-listed edifice has been restored in a £5.8 million project to provide a heritage centre and prestigious office accommodation. One hundred years, that is how long Govan was to be the centre of shipbuilding on the River Clyde, in Scotland. The finest vessels, steamships and the most luxurious liners would grace the area from design to the official launch.

Welcome my friends to Govan's Fairfield Shipyard and our next focal point for paranormal public investigations across Scotland. Built on Govan Road between 1889 and 1891 the new block of offices was functional, with ship and engine drawing offices on the first floor, feeding drawings to the engine works, to the west, and to the mould loft, to the east, where the lines of the vessels were drawn out in full-scale. The ground floor was occupied by managers' offices, and by a boardroom, which was also used to entertain clients, for instance at launch parties. It is these lower levels that we will be focussing on fully as we look for the energies that still wander this location.

The activity at this location is very similar to the activity along the road at the Pearce Institute, a location we have investigated extensively. Not only this, the locations are linked by the same historical characters. Much like the Pearce Institute, this location has been subject to strange activity witnessed by staff and visitors alike. Lights turning on and off, ghostly figures said to have been witnessed floating through the corridors and rooms and unexplained environmental changes such as temperature and static energy.

Perhaps some of the artefacts within the building also contain energy? On more than one occasion whilst investigating here up in the attic area I have witnessed three separate mediums pick up on the feeling of strangling of a rope around there neck believing possibly someone may have taken their own life in this area. With it being such a busy working environment there is no surprise to have the feelings of pain. Stories do suggest some unfortunate workers injuring themselves on machinery and untimely losing their lives. One thing for sure the Govan shipyard building days might be a thing of the past but are kept alive by this fantastic piece of history that will live on long past us.

"A place full of so much history and character you can almost see and feel the works happening 100 years later"

A. Reid 18/09/2018

The Govan Shipyard Breakfast

This recipe was created and inspired by Alister Reid to the shipbuilders of Govan from years gone by

Ingredients
300g Floury Potatoes
40g Unsalted Butter
60g Plain Flour
1/2 Teaspoon Baking Powder
Smoked Scottish Salmon
Free Range Eggs
Cherry Vine Tomatoes
Chives

Method
Peel and roughly chop the potatoes, cook in gently boiling salted water until tender. Drain, then put back into the pan and gently heat for a few minutes to evaporate more moisture, then mash with the butter. Combine the flour, baking powder and a good pinch of salt in a bowl. Add the warm mash to the flour mixture and combine gently with a spoon to make a dough. Carefully shape the dough into two balls and transfer to a lightly floured surface. Roll each ball into a circle about 6 mm thick, and then cut into quarters. Heat a heavy pan over medium heat. Once hot, add a little oil, carefully place the potato scones into the pan and cook for two to three minutes on each side, or until golden brown. Serve the potato scones with chive scrambled eggs and slices of smoked Scottish salmon and top with grilled cherry vine tomatoes and garnish with some fresh rocket lettuce.

The Wizard of Balwearie, Sir Michael Scott

Sitting on the south side of Kirkcaldy are the ruins of Balwearie Castle, said to once have been the home of Michael Scott, a notorious and feared wizard and sorcerer, better known as the Wizard of Balwearie.

Known most commonly as the Wizard of the North, a title given to him by Sir Walter Scott centuries after Michael Scott's death, Sir Walter researched him extensively and would even go on to write a poem about the Wizard. Feared by many for his reported magical powers, Michael Scott was a noted mathematician and philosopher who achieved international renown for his intellect and wizardly skills.

Not much is known about the early life of the great wizard or if he was even ever born in Kirkcaldy, some research suggests he may have been born in Durham; however it is documented he was born around 1175. He completed his studies in Durham and then in Oxford and Paris. Later he travelled to the great Toledo Cathedral in Spain, where he was engaged in translating several books and scripts from Arabic to Latin. It's not certain exactly when he returned to Scotland, but most likely it was around or after 1220.

One such tale of Scott's powers tells that in the time of King Alexander III reign, Scotland along with its ships was under attack from French pirates. King Alexander ordered the Wizard to go and visit the King of France to request the immediate cessation of the attacks. Scott set out on his quest, visited France and returned home in only one night, a feat that would have been near impossible in today's times never mind the 13th Century. He is said to have climbed to the top of nearby Bell Crag, a rocky red stone outcrop close to his castle where he was reported to practice and use his crafts and magical powers. It was a place that had always been described as mystical even before the wizard had returned to Scotland.

He was often seen traveling on his way to Bell Crag regularly on a large black oversized horse, claimed to be the horse of a demon due to its great size and incredible strength. Below Bell Crag, there was a deep cave. Scott would stand above the cave and use what was best described as a funnel of energetic warm air that would twist itself up and out of a hole in the cave roof, allowing a platform for Scott to cast his spells. It was a place where Heaven and Hell both existed, a place where he would recharge his powers and summon his Demons. Local folklore claims that he could summon his Demons on demand - did he use them to build his castles and do his work? Despite all this, it was never overtly known if he would use dark magic as such, but I guess it was a chilling reminder to many that he could and would if he needed.

Rumours of Bell Crag described as the place where you could foresee the future, a place Scott had foreseen his own death, wherein he would be struck on the head by a falling stone or masonry. From the day of him foreseeing his own death, he would venture out with extra precautions wearing a metal helmet when leaving his castle and buildings. One fateful day whilst attending his local church, a place where all men are expected to and required to remove their hats, he stepped out of the church only to be hit on the head by a falling stone. The stone itself was not big enough to cause instant death. It only caused a small cut that later became infected, and the infection spread throughout his body. He would die just a few days later. It would appear the prophecy became true and he had fulfilled what he had witnessed at Bell Crag.

The exact burial location of Michael Scott is not known although he is believed to be buried in the Scottish borders. Melrose seems to be the location of his grave, he is believed to be buried with his spellbook so it would not fall into the wrong hands and would hopefully be long forgotten about due to the potential dangers and powers it may bring. It's believed through secret knowledge, the book and Scott were buried with a cross to stave off the demons who worked for him and to prevent any further possible conflict from his grave. As Scoot was a man who was said to have had so much power, it's no wonder that these precautions were taken seriously and strongly. The Wizard may no longer be around, but the reminders and stories of his reign are still present, and his legend lives on.

Not much is now left of Balwearie Castle other than the remaining wall and half turret ruins. Ghostly tales of the area are said to still lurk, including a phantom piper close to Bell Crag; ghostly servants are still seen within and around the castle ruins almost continuing their work. Who knows, but it may be that Michael Scott "the wizard of Balwearie" is one of the spirits lurking at his once intimidating home.

"An overwhelming feeling of magic."

A.Reid 20/09/19

The Wizards Porridge

This recipe was created by Alister Reid to the Wizard of Balwearie

Ingredients
100g Scottish Porridge Oats
200ml Full Fat Milk
2 Organic Leeks
4 Banana Shallots
200g Unsalted Butter
30g Crispy Pancetta Lardons
1 Arbroath Smokie
20g Finely Grated Parmesan
Salt/Pepper
Chives

Method
Bring a large pan of water to the boil, wash and then finely slice leeks and plunge into the boiling water. Boil for two minutes then strain and plunge into iced water. Drain again and squeeze gently to remove some of the retained water out of the leeks, add to a food processor and blitz until smooth. The leeks should be thick in texture and a very vibrant green colour. Fold the leek puree into the softened butter until the butter is green and you have a nice leek butter. Set aside until later, finely dice the shallots and sweat in a pre-heated pan with a little olive oil. For maximum flavour add in the pancetta raw at this stage and cook until crispy and the shallots are translucent, otherwise, fry the pancetta in a separate pan and add in later to the porridge. Then add the porridge to the pan and add in milk slowly and gradually. You may not need all the milk or may require a little more depending on the quality of the oats. When you have an almost thick porridge consistency add in a few spoonfuls of the leek butter (the rest can be kept in the refrigerator for a week for future use) and fold into the porridge. This will loosen the oats and make a nice creamy risotto texture and spread nicely when plated. Fold in the picked and boneless smokie, Stir in the parmesan, season to taste with salt and pepper, add in the chives and serve. It can be nice served as a little savoury starter, garnish with crispy leeks and baby herbs.

Dunino Den & the Druid Gods

Nestled in the hillside forest behind Dunino Church, lies the ancient Pre-Christian place of worship, Dunino Den. Surrounded in mystery this was once an important worship site. The den is still visited today by Modern Pagans and Christians. people will leave offerings such as ribbons, coins, and crystals to name, but a few offerings that are present here. With the beliefs of good luck and prosperity associated with the place, white witches practise crafts and rituals here, with the safety of the ancient gods surrounding them and also protecting the worship site. You will find many important carvings and symbols carved into the rock walls just adding to the atmospheric feelings within the den, important messages, ancient myths and meanings, including the face of the Green Man, just to add to that little bit more to the already historical site.

Green Man Dunino Den

First thought to have been used around 4000BC, druids were the most highly spiritually advanced people in ancient Scotland; Druidism was driven underground by the fear of persecution from the Christian missionaries. It's not known why the Druids would choose such a site for a place of worship, but it could have been to do with the sun and the dark: the dark surroundings would allow the sun to beam in on the site to allow the gods and worshippers to venerate the light of the sun and the energy it creates.

One of the main altars at Dunino

There are two main crags within the den one, which would appear to be the main altar - this is perched high overlooking the Den. The other crag consists of a sacrificial pool with a footprint pressed into the rock beside the pool. It was most likely this was used for animal sacrifices; with the stream below flowing past, they would place the dead within the river to be washed away and effectively back into the earth. Stories suggest it might have been used for human sacrifices but there is no strong evidence to suggest this. If standing beside the pool with your foot inside the carved footprint, local legend says to be careful what you wish for as it will come true. It is possible the footprint might be symbolic, and it is completely possible that kings might have been crowned here with Royal ceremonies perhaps associated with the site.

Dunino Church just above the den was likely built upon a stone circle, with some of the stones being used in the fabrication of the church. These can still be seen within the church walls. Other stories report that the stone circle might have been on the other side of Dunino altogether, but it was not uncommon for churches to be built on old pagan worship sites. It was also likely the church was built and placed here to show power over the ancient pre-Christian religion.

Dunino Church

Ancient stories tell of fairies haunting the den along with other strange and scary creatures or beings within the Celtic legends of encounters. Stepping down the thousands of years old worn steps is literally a step back in time. Whilst in the Den there is always a feeling of being watched and the feelings of curiosity, the Den has links to Witches, the Picts and still present rituals taking place, with such an ancient history who knows what else has visited the den and taken place.

"Strong beliefs will never truly be forgotten, ignore the cover-ups and follow your own beliefs"

A.Reid 14/01/18

Celtic Shortbread of Dunino Den

This recipe was created by Alister Reid to remember the ancient worship site

Celtic shortbread

Ingredients

225g Unsalted Softened Butter
110g Caster Sugar
225g Plain Flour
110g Cornflour
Few Sprigs Thyme
2 Tbsp. Lavender Honey
Little Lemon Zest
½ Tsp Vanilla Bean Paste
Pinch Of Salt

Method

Mix flour, sugar, cornflour, and salt in a large bowl. Pick the leaves of the thyme and sprinkle into the dry mixture dispose of the stalks. Grate the lemon zest into the flour. In a separate bowl, place the butter, honey, and vanilla then tip into the flour. Rub the butter mixture in together with the flour using your fingertips until all combined and resembling a breadcrumb texture. Tip out onto a lightly floured surface and combine into a dough. Do not overmix. Wrap in cling film and place in the refrigerator for at least one hour or until needed. This will allow the shortbread to rest and develop its flavour. Remove from the refrigerator and allow to soften slightly then turn out onto a lightly floured surface and roll to 2-3cm thick. Cut into rounds or fingers and transfer to a none stick baking tray leaving space between them for expansion. Bake at 190°C for around 18-20 minutes or until lightly golden leave to cool on trays and serve with a nice cup of fruit flavoured tea.

Pluscarden Abbey & the Wolf of Badenoch

Pluscarden Abbey

Pluscarden Abbey is situated six miles southeast of Elgin, Moray. The Abbey is a Roman Catholic Benedict Monastery; Alexander the II founded it in 1230 for the Valliscaulian Order. Pluscarden is one of the oldest Medieval working monasteries in Great Britain. At present 18 monks live and work within the Abbey. The etymology of Pluscarden is possibly Pictish, but it is not fully known or understood. It even could be the abstraction of two words from two different languages the first being Pictish and the latter from early Gaelic perhaps meaning an "enclosure" or a "place". Whatever it means or represents it is most definitely from an ancient language or the beginning of a new language. The Abbey has seen many changes over the centuries, most noticeably during the years of the Scottish Reformation, which saw a decline within the Priory and by the 1680s, it was in a ruinous condition. After lying derelict for years, some work was done in the 19th century to arrest the decay of the building and save its future.

The Wolf

MP Lord Colum Crichton-Stuart who would go on to own the lands and buildings at Pluscarden gave the Priory and its lands to the Benedictine Prinknash Abbey in 1943. The newfound community began to arrive in early 1948 and within seven years, the church's bell tower had been roofed. Restoration work continued for the next 20 years and in 1966, the priory obtained its independence from Prinknash, achieving abbey status in 1974. The Abbey was now back in operation after its long exodus and was a working monastery as we see it today. The Abbey welcomes guests and conducts formal retreats. Silence is observed in the Church, Refectory and other monastic areas. Guests often help with the manual work of the Abbey, alongside the Monks.

During the earlier years of the Abbey, a name would become very highly associated with the Monastery but not for the reasons of good causes. This person was Alexander Stewart, born 1314; he was the Earl of Buchanan, also fiercely named "The Wolf of Badenoch". No evidence suggests he was given this name during his reign and lifetime, with many claiming it was given to him in later centuries long after his death. Alexander is best remembered for his brutal destruction and Hell fire-raising of the royal burgh of Elgin and its famous Cathedral, forests and Pluscarden Abbey. His nickname was earned due to his notorious cruelty and rapacity. He would burn down and destroy much of Pluscarden Abbey, leaving his trace on the Monastery that can be seen today.

He was the illegitimate and third surviving son of King Robert II of Scotland. He was for a short time the *Justiciar of Scotia* (in Norman-Latin, *Justiciarus Scotie*) was the most senior legal office in the High Medieval Kingdom of Scotland. *Scotia* (meaning Scotland). However, he was not to be an effective one. He held many large territories in the north of Scotland but would eventually go on to lose a large amount of these. His main residence, the "Wolf's Lair": was Lochindorb Castle at Lochindorb in Badenoch, a stronghold of Alexander for much of his reign.

He also held Ruthven Castle, now Ruthven Barracks. With such a brutal reputation it's no surprise some of the stories we are told about the "Wolf" are nasty. He is believed to have practised witchcraft and the darker side of the magic during the dark hours of the night with his followers! One night, he is said to have played or challenged the devil to a game of poker or possibly even chess at Ruthven Castle and ultimately won the game and beat the devil!

Ultimately, the devil was unhappy at his loss and sent Stewart's castle and all his men including The Wolf himself to perish into a burning inferno! The following morning The Wolf was found in his banqueting hall with his body completely unmarked although the nails in his boots had been pulled out and vanished, perhaps the perils for playing cards with the devil. It's said on dark and stormy nights, a small group of men in cloaks can be seen in a dark corner continuing their game, with the devil is regularly present. Despite so much power and credibility, it would appear The Wolf was no match for Auld Nick. His body is laid to rest at Dunkeld cathedral.

"Such a peaceful place, where all your worries disappear for a time. The rage is the wolf upon leaving"

A. Reid 11/01/19

The Wolf's Benedict

This recipe was created by Alister Reid to commemorate the re-establishment of Pluscarden Abbey

The Wolf's Benedict

Ingredients
200g Unsalted Softened Butter
100ml White Wine Vinegar
4 Free Range Egg Yolks
6 Free Range Eggs
6 White Peppercorns
Few Sprigs Thyme
Few Sprigs Dill

6 Slices Honey Roast Ham
3 Breakfast Muffins
Bunch New Season Asparagus

Method

Slowly clarify the butter over low heat. Place 60ml of the vinegar into a pan with the thyme, dill, and peppercorns; reduce on the heat by half. Set aside to cool slightly. Separate four eggs and place yolks into a steel bowl. Fill a pan with cold water and bring to a rolling boil turn down the heat to a simmer and place the steel bowl with egg yolks on top - make sure the water does not touch the bowl. Gently whisk the egg yolks until they begin to form soft ribbons. Strain the vinegar to remove the dill, peppercorns, and thyme and slowly begin to pour in the reduced vinegar to the egg yolks while still whisking vigorously until the mixture begins to once again thicken slightly. You may need to remove the bowl from the pot from time to time so you do not scramble the egg, then begin to gently treacle in the clarified butter continuing to whisk vigorously until the pale and creamy sauce has been made (Hollandaise Sauce). Set aside the sauce in a warm but gentle heat until ready to serve. Break the bottoms of the asparagus where they snap and peel the ends to nice points, bring the water to a rolling boil and place in the asparagus for one to two minutes and then remove from water and place asparagus into an ice bath. Then add the remaining vinegar to the water and bring to a gentle simmer, cut the muffins in half and toast until golden brown, spread with generous amounts of butter. Gently crack the eggs into the simmering water and cook until soft and still runny for around two to three minutes. Whilst this is happening, bring a pan of salted water to the boil and place the asparagus in it to warm through then strain the water from the asparagus and the eggs. Let eggs rest on a paper towel to firm slightly and drain any excess water. Top buttered muffins with the asparagus and then the ham, place eggs on top and cover with spoonfuls of the Hollandaise Sauce. Serve immediately with some cracked black pepper and chopped fresh garden herbs.

The Legend of Regulus, St Andrews and the Boar

St Andrews Harbour

Saint Regulus or Saint Rule was a 4th century monk or bishop of Patras, Greece, who in AD 345 is said to have fled to Scotland with the bones of Saint Andrew, and deposited them at St Andrews. Regulus kept the relics, which consisted of three fingers from the right hand, three toes, an arm bone, a tooth and a kneecap of St Andrew, kept hidden in a small chest, which St Regulus had constructed for the purpose of storing the relics, while he awaited further instruction from the angels.

A little while later, St Regulus had another vision in which an angel instructed him to gather a small and trusted crew, to set sail from Greece with the relics of St Andrew immediately. St Regulus was instructed to sail west, to the end of the earth, where he should establish a church dedicated to St Andrew. St Regulus did as instructed, and with a small crew of seventeen monks and three nuns, he left Patras on the dangerous voyage, during which he had no idea where or when he would end up.

They travelled across the Mediterranean Sea, through the Strait of Gibraltar, around the coasts of Spain, France and into the English Channel then onto the North Sea where, after an estimated two years at sea, a violent storm drove them ashore and they were shipwrecked on the coast of Pictland (as Scotland was known then). Seeking shelter from the storm, St Regulus and the crew found a deep cave in the towering cliffs, situated between where the castle and harbour now exist, where they took the chest containing the relics. At that time, the country was predominantly still under the rule of the Picts, who are often depicted as being primitive and barbaric in their way of life. The truth is however that the Picts did not keep written records, and so much about them was written by those who arrived and sought to stamp out their religions, resulting in the writing being far from favourable.

The area that St Regulus found himself was known as Muckross, meaning Land of the Boars, and with dense forests and deep bogs, it is difficult to imagine how different the landscape was to that now seen in and around St Andrews. There, woodlands were overrun with wild boar, of such size and ferocity that some of the first accounts compare them to the Erymanthian Boar, the capture of which was the fourth labour of Hercules. The land was ruled by the Pictish King Hergust from Abernethy, the Capital of his Kingdom and, upon hearing what had happened, the King travelled to Muckross to see for himself.

Just before the consecration of Bishop Robert, an important but forgotten event took place. King Alexander I granted an important, valuable and well-known district of land to the Church of St Andrew. This section of land, which extended from St Andrews to the current village of Boarhills, had previously been removed from the Church for an undisclosed reason, yet King Alexander offered to restore the rights of the Church on the land, on the condition that religion was fixed as ordained by King Alexander. The land generated considerable revenue, yet there was one issue - it was the territory of a massive wild boar, which had been responsible for killing cattle and men over the years.

Several huntsmen had tried and failed, to hunt down and kill the boar, which led to the area being known as Boar's Chace. Eventually, a group of hunters was sent out who were successful in capturing and killing the boar. The official Coat of Arms of St Andrews shows the image of St Andrew

64

holding his cross on one side, and a large boar chained to an oak tree on the other, and early historical reports indicate that it was the capture of the boar at Boar's Chace that inspired the image of the boar.

Fish Market

"St. Andrews is my most favourite place in the world and in my honest opinion one of the most haunted towns in the world"

A.Reid 23/09/19

Saint Andrews Spicy Cullen Skink

This recipe was created by Alister Reid to Saint Regulus and Saint Andrew

Ingredients
2 White Onions
4 Large Leeks
20g Chicken Stock
2 Natural Smoked Haddock Fillets
400ml Double Cream
2 Picante Chorizo Sausage
2 Rooster Potatoes
Bunch of Chives
Milk
Salt
Pepper

Method
Firstly, peel the Rooster Potatoes and cut into small one-centimetre cubes. Place in a pot and cover with cold water, add a pinch of salt and bring to a gentle rolling boil for 10-12 minutes or until tender but still Al Dente. Remove from the heat and run under cold water until cool, drain and set aside. Cut down the middle of the leeks but leaving the root attached, turn over and cut again so you have four sections, but leave the root bottom of leek still attached. Rinse under cold running water to clean then shred finely. Bring a pot of salted water to the boil and blanch the leeks until just cooked, refresh under cold water, drain and again set aside until ready, place the smoked haddock fillets into a pan and cover with milk. Bring to a gentle boil and turn the heat off, leave the Haddock to infuse the milk and cool in the liquid. Dice the onions finely, heat a heavy-based pan, dice the chorizo into small chunks and place into the pan. Sweat slightly to allow the oils to release then add the onions and sweat off until translucent. Add the cream to the pot along with the milk drained from the haddock fillets. Make up chicken stock with 100ml boiling water, add this to the pan and bring the pan to a gentle boil to reduce slightly and thicken, add in the leeks, potato, and chunky flaked haddock, warm through, adjust seasoning accordingly to personal taste and serve with a sprinkle of chopped chives. The addition of crispy bacon lardons is also a nice addition. I serve this with a warm cheese scone and butter, a real nice hearty dish

Newark Castle and the Old Kirk Ghost

Newark Castle

Newark Castle is situated close to the historic fishing village of St Monans, in the East Nuek of Fife. Newark Castle is an Ancient Scheduled Monument ruin, located just outside the town of St Monans and probably dates back to at least the 13th century. Not much is known about the castle and its possible its name or names before the 15th century. It is noted that King Alexander III is believed to have spent a large part of his childhood at this location. The castle sits proudly on the coastline, with dramatic views looking out over the North Sea. Further along the Fife coastal path are the few remains of Ardoss Castle. It is closely linked to St Monans Auld Kirk, which itself, dates back to around the year 875 when Saint Monan was buried there. Secrets and local tales tell of a possible secret tunnel located deep beneath the castles possibly linking the two locations together, no evidence has ever been found of this, but the rumours still live on in the local community.

The current castle was constructed in the early 15th century by the Kinloch family, it then passed, through marriage, to the Sandilands of Cruivie, who would sell the castle to one of its most famous owners, David Leslie in 1649. Leslie was a prominent figure in the English and Scottish Civil Wars, becoming Lord Newark after the Wars had ended. Following on from Leslie's death in 1682, the castle would be passed to the local Anstruther family, and finally to the Bairds of Elie, again local ownership from the area.

The castle was eventually abandoned in the 19th century and quickly fell into the ruinous condition it is now in, the castle has suffered badly from coastal erosion. Despite this, there are still accessible vaulted cellars within the castle but these are dangerous and should not be entered or you enter at your own risk. The castle was given one more possible chance and a potential new lease of life in the early 1990s when a Canadian millionaire purchased the ruins and grounds. Unfortunately with it being a Scheduled ancient ruin it had to remain in this condition and was unable to be rebuilt to its glorious former self and remains in decline today.

Paranormal activity is present here. The story I want to share with you for this location is an extremely fascinating one and a story I've known since I was a child, despite only visiting the castle for the first time as an adult. On a particular winters evening, one that was extraordinarily dark and silent, a young boy was conducting his cleaning duties within the old nearby historical Kirk of St Monans. He was nearly done for the evening; the last of his duties was cleaning out the old ash from the furnace before he locked up the church and headed home for the evening. On his exit, the young boy glanced back at the church, and saw an all-mighty flash of light from the darkness of the old Kirk's Tower, lighting up the gloomy, dark atmosphere. Much to his astonishment, he witnessed a pale looking face shining back towards him, from within the Tower.

It was at this point that he ran to the nearby Minister's home as fast as he could. When he got there, his astonishment and shock were to increase, as a portrait hanging on the wall at the home of the Minister was identical that of the apparition he just witnessed at the Tower. The young lad had just witnessed the St Monans Auld Kirk Ghost first-hand. It was Sir David Leslie of Newark, the long-dead previous owner of the nearby Newark Castle.

"I'm unsure of my exact draw to this castle, it could be a possible ancient family line, whatever it is, it's one of

my favourite places and locations to visit"

A.Reid 22/03/19

Newark's Shepherd's Pie
This recipe was created by Alister Reid to honour the remains of Newark Castle

Ingredients
2 Large Onions
2 Medium Carrots
100g Fresh Garden Peas
500g Minced Black Face Lamb
3 Tbsp. Tomato Puree
2 Tbsp. Worcestershire Sauce
2 Tbsp. Brown Sauce
Fresh Thyme Sprigs
100ml Lamb Stock
200ml Peeled Chopped Tomatoes
Sunflower Oil
800g Mashed Potato
200g Mashed Parsnips
Few Sprigs Thyme
Few Sprigs Rosemary
100g Unsalted Butter
100ml Double Cream
Salt
Pepper

Method
Preheat oven to 180°C. Place the pie dish into the oven to heat up. Heat a little oil in a large heavy pan, add the diced onions, cook over medium heat, until translucent and beginning to brown, add in the grated carrot, thyme, and rosemary, cover the pan and cookout for a few minutes. Remove the vegetables from the pan and add in the lamb meat, cook until browned, then add the tomato puree, chopped tomatoes, stock, brown sauce, Worcester sauce. Bring to the boil, then reduce the heat and simmer for one to two hours, stirring continuously so it does not stick to the bottom of the pan. Peel the potatoes and parsnips. Chop the potatoes into quarters and place in a pot, cut the stalk centres from the parsnips and discard, cut parsnips into large chunks and place in a pot beside the potatoes, cover with water and add in a pinch of salt, bring to the boil then reduce heat. Simmer for 15-20 minutes or until potatoes and parsnips are soft. Drain, then mash with the butter and the cream. Season with salt and pepper, and set aside. When the lamb bolognaise is ready to pour, add it in with the peas and mix into the mixture, spoon the lamb mixture into the pie dish, then carefully put spoonfuls of mash over the lamb mixture, Smooth it over and with a fork create furrows on the top. Bake the shepherd's pie for

30–40 minutes or until the top is browned and crispy, serve with garlic bread and a helping of roasted root vegetables

1B Westport Cupar - The War Widow

1B Westport, Cupar

For the final and 13th recipe, it is my lucky number 13, so it's only fitting I dedicate this recipe to my business and livelihood. 1B Westport was established by myself in 2014 and still going strong; we are a family ran business dedicated to homemade food, cakes, and award-winning coffee.

Interestingly enough, for this building to be haunted or considered haunted would perhaps bat an eyelid or two. The current building is only eight years old! It was built from scratch by my father-in-law and is a classic three-story structure consisting of the café on the ground floor and en suite rooms on the upper storeys. Before this, the land contained a large garage used by the local vets to park their cars and even carry out their lambing season within.

1B Westport is located in the historic market town of Cupar, in Fife. A former main county Burgh, there are records of civilisation dating back to well before the Bronze Age 4000 years ago. It is a town with many former tollbooths and even a former prison. It also had its own Gallows where death sentences would be offered in front of a bemused crowd of several thousand. Secret tunnels run across the town, with underground sewers running the length of St Catharine's Street right up through the Bonnygate, up to the Westport area.

One story of the town's darker tales talks about two young men sentenced to death for murder being taken from the old prison via an underground tunnel through the town to the hanging gallows. Ten thousand members of the public gathered on a beautiful summer morning to witness the towns last ever hangings almost 160 years ago. The date was 1852, when brothers Michael and Peter Scanlin would be publicly hanged after being found guilty of slaying 66-year-old Margaret Maxwell.

One of the local Cuperarians, stated, "It's a braw day for a hanging". Miss Maxwell was found lying dead in her small bread and meal shop on the morning of February 16th, 1852. She had been struck over the head with a stool causing her to fall to her unfortunate death. Police were quick to turn their attention to the brothers who had come from Ireland to Scotland to seek railway work. But when the work dried up began a savage campaign of crime across the town. They stole Margaret Maxwell's watch and money before scarpering.

Incidentally and perhaps unfortunate for the brothers they had been residing only just next door to Miss Maxwell. With their names already hot throughout the town they were arrested immediately. Both brothers had a reputation for being decidedly 'cocky and arrogant'. In fact, upon their arrest and charging, Michael would comment to the police "You'll have to prove that, Sir".

However, their attitude quickly changed when their close and one-time friend would testify against them and tell police everything. They were soon to be facing the dreaded noose. It took only fifteen minutes for the jury to deliver the guilty verdict and the bothers would face their fate on July the 5th 1852, being sentenced to hanging by the neck until dead.

The execution took place at what is now the Fluthers car park, across from the old town jail. Special gallows were brought from Edinburgh by train for the execution. Owing to a fear that a group of Irishmen would storm the gallows and try to free the brothers, as a precaution, a detachment of foot soldiers, cavalry and 200 special constables were brought in to deter any possible rescue attempt.

A full four hours before the event, the crowds gathered in their thousands, Michael and Peter were visited by a local priest before being taken to the gallows. Asked if they would forgive their executioner they both replied, "Yes" and touchingly hugged each other before the hoods were put over their heads, the brothers protested their innocence until the end but on that fateful morning, it would be all over by 8.15 am - it was the town's last execution.

Cupar has much rich history, even records of royalty and visits within the last two centuries was not an uncommon theme for public events within the town. One of the world's oldest nine-hole golf courses is located on the outer side of the town uniquely on a sloping hill making it a challenging course for even the professional. At least two ancient castles are recorded, one being Castlehill now the site of Castlehill Primary School and also a castle at Moathill, directly opposite 1B Westport. This is one of the areas I will focus on in relation to possible hauntings within the Westport. The castle was built by the Earls of Fife and was ultimately known as Cupar Castle. Records suggest the first foundations were laid in or around the 11th century.

The castle was surrendered to the English in 1296 and King Edward I of England would stay in the castle for a long period. In 1306, Robert Wishart

(Bishop of Glasgow) a supporter of the Wars of Scottish Independence, William Wallace and King Robert the Bruce, he would lead Scottish forces to besiege the castle, taking it back into the hands of its rightful owners. However, the attack cost Wishart his freedom as he was caught in Cupar by the English forces after the attack. The castle then fell into decline and is no longer visible other than parts of the defensive walls and moat; recent excavations found charcoaled bones that had been carbonated and thought to be some 4000 years old, many weapons parts and coins were also discovered during the works carried out.

Cupar Castle would lead me to part of the story of a possible connection to paranormal activity within the Westport foundations. After doing some research, I was able to find and prove there was a building on the site of the Westport obviously now long gone that dated back at least a century or possibly more.

Within the five years of me owning the shop my staff and I have witnessed our fair share of phenomena, such as lights going on and off, shadows, knocks, feelings of being watched, things disappearing and then reappearing, and ghostly whispers, I myself have witnessed an item moving for no apparent or possibly explainable reason. One story of such an event occurred in the morning ahead of a busy day before opening: a staff member was on the top landing with me on the ground floor. The staff member came back down to ask what I had been shouting up the stairs, which I would deny, as it was not me or any other physical human. She claimed it was a male's voice but perhaps not my own. The whole time I had been through the back in the kitchen prepping. This is where the strange thing would occur. I heard a female voice shouting through the doorway at me! Moreover, I had believed it to be my staff member, which she would deny. Other reports include that of a young girl running around the shop floor only to disappear on approach, and guest reporting pictures falling from the wall (always the same picture).

There is nothing sinister here at all; it's all extremely friendly and peaceful. I would just describe the spirits as playful. But the story I would personally like to share with you is my wartime lady. I will not name names as, in my opinion, it is too soon and I would like to remain respectful to not only her but also her possible still living family.

Many people have often asked who the friendly but sad lady is upstairs. This is who we believe to be an Italian lady from the war period. She is waiting and looking for her husband to come home from war, but unfortunately, it would appear her beloved did not return and ultimately she would die from a broken heart. She is still filled with much sadness and is waiting with the hope that her husband will one day return. We managed to find the names and it matched the local war memorial records and backed up our beliefs are and who this lady might well be. She is sad but happy to be here I guess. This also proves in paranormal research that it is not necessarily the building present that's haunted but the land itself and structures that have been there before.

Another possible explanation for so much activity is that of an ancient well within the foundations or the surrounding area, that was once possibly part of the local castle. Is this perhaps a travel system for spirits? Many suggest that water is a conductor and almost like a ley line for spirit travel. Whatever the activity around us it's meant to be and we live happily together.

"One day I hope to find all the history I need within my own backyard"

A.Reid 23/09/19

1B Westport Salted Caramel Banana Pancake Stack

This recipe was created by Alister Reid. 1B is famous for pancakes and this is our secret family recipe

Westport Banana Pancakes

Ingredients
8 Large Free-Range Eggs
750g Self Raising Flour
365g Caster Sugar
3 Tsp Bicarbonate Soda
Semi Skimmed Milk
6 Bananas
Nutella
Toffee Sauce
Micro Fudge

80g Unsalted Butter
150g Light Sift Brown Sugar
Sea Salt Flakes
700ml Double Cream
300ml Milk
1 Vanilla Pod
3 Free Range Egg Yolks

Pancakes in the making

Method

In a large metal bowl, crack the eight whole eggs. Weigh out the flour, 250g caster sugar and bicarbonate, gently combine the mixture in a mixing machine slowly adding in the desired amount of milk until smooth and thick but pourable texture, refrigerate for at least one hour. For the ice cream, pour 300ml of milk and 300ml cream into a tall heavy-based pan. Strip the vanilla pod and seeds, place into the mixture, and gently bring to the boil then turn off. In a metal bowl, whisk the three egg yolks and 115g caster sugar together until pale and creamy. Gently pour over the warm cream mixture, whisking vigorously until it is all incorporated and being careful not to scramble the eggs. Chill over an ice bath. When cool place in an ice-cream churner and churn until ready. Normally this takes 45 minutes. In another heavy-based tall pan add the butter, brown sugar and 300ml cream, heat gently over moderate heat until boiling. Turn down slightly and whisk for 20 minutes until it is all smooth. Add a sprinkle of sea salt and set aside. When ready to use gently ladle out round pancakes to your required or desired size. Let them bubble and when ready flip over to reveal a nice golden brown pancake. Cook the remaining side down until cooked through, spread generously with Nutella. Place on a metal tray slice and lay the bananas out, and cover with a sprinkling of caster sugar, then blow torch until caramelised, when cool using a pallet knife, layer the bananas over the Nutella pancakes, and stack on top of each other, usually three in a stack. Scoop two balls of fresh vanilla ice cream and place on top of the pancake, drizzle with warm salted toffee sauce, serve, and enjoy.

Thinking of the next investigation...or recipe!

Made in the USA
Coppell, TX
11 December 2024

42193671R00049